Shaquille O'Neal

BASKETBALL SUPERSTAR

Josepha Sherman

P.O. Box 196
Hockessin, Delaware 19707
Visit us on the web: www.mitchelllane.com
Comments? email us: mitchelllane@mitchelllane.com

A Robbie Reader

Albert Einstein	Alex Rodriguez	Barbara Park
Charles Schulz	Dale Earnhardt Jr.	Donovan McNabb
Dr. Seuss	Henry Ford	Hilary Duff
Jamie Lynn Spears	Johnny Gruelle	LeBron James
Mia Hamm	Philo T. Farnsworth	Robert Goddard
Shaquille O'Neal	The Story of Harley-Davidson	Syd Hoff
Thomas Edison	Tony Hawk	

Library of Congress Cataloging-in-Publication Data
Sherman, Josepha.
    Shaquille O'Neal / by Josepha Sherman.
        p. cm. — (A Robbie reader)
    Includes bibliographical references and index.
    ISBN 1-58415-361-X (library bound)
    1. O'Neal, Shaquille—Juvenile literature. 2. Basketball players—United States—Juvenile literature. I. Title. II. Series.
GV884.O54S45 2005
796.323'092—dc22
                                                        2004030521

ABOUT THE AUTHOR: Josepha Sherman is a professional fantasy and science fiction writer, a Star Trek novelist, a children's book writer, and a nonfiction writer with over 60 books in print. She is also a professional folklorist and editor. In addition, she is a native New Yorker, has a degree in archaeology, loves to tinker with computers, follows the NY Mets, and is a horse whisperer who has had a new foal fall asleep on her foot!

PHOTO CREDITS: Cover, p. 18—Reuters; p. 4—Don Ryan/AP Photo; pp. 6, 11, 14—Chris O'Meara/AP Photo; p. 8—Victor Spinell/WireImage; p. 12—Bill Haber/AP Photo; p. 16—Steve Simoneau/AP Photos; p. 20—Matt Sayles/AP Photo; p. 21—Julie Jacobson/AP Photo; pp. 22, 24—Steve Granitz/WireImage; p. 27 (top)—John Heller/WireImage; p. 27 (bottom)—J. Pat Carter/AP Photo.

ACKNOWLEDGMENTS: The following story has been thoroughly researched, and to the best of our knowledge, represents a true story. While every possible effort has been made to ensure accuracy, the publisher will not assume liability for damages caused by inaccuracies in the data, and makes no warranty on the accuracy of the information contained herein. This story has not been authorized nor endorsed by anyone associated with Shaquille O'Neal.

TABLE OF CONTENTS

Chapter One
The Rookie Star 5

Chapter Two
Early Years 9

Chapter Three
Basketball Pro 13

Chapter Four
Champion 17

Chapter Five
Father, Actor, and Rapper 23

Chronology 28
Selected Discography 29
Selected Filmography 29
Career Shooting Stats 29
Find Out More 30
Glossary 31
Index 32

The NBA Draft is when new players are picked by the professional basketball teams. In June 1992, while Shaquille O'Neal was still in college at Louisiana State University, he was picked by the Orlando Magic. He later did get his college degree.

The Rookie Star

The crowd of basketball fans sat forward. Shaquille O'Neal, newest member of the Orlando Magic, was entering the game. He was only a **rookie**, but he was over seven feet tall and weighed over three hundred pounds. Shaq had once stopped a game by accident. While **making a basket**, he had pulled down the basketball hoop and its supporting backboard. That move became known as the Shaq Attack.

The first player to face Shaq tried to get past him. Shaq calmly hit the basketball away. Then Shaq had a chance to get the ball. He went right by the opposing team players as though they weren't there. At the **basket**, one player tried to block him. Shaq just reached up over him and dunked the ball right through the

Felton Spencer (right) of the Utah Jazz tries to stop Shaq from shooting a basket. But Shaq is already out of his reach and going for a slam dunk. Shaq probably doesn't realize that he's sticking out his tongue!

hoop. As the game went on, he did that again and again.

When the game was over, the Orlando Magic had won. Shaq had scored over 26 points. Now the crowd knew that they had seen a rising basketball star.

Shaq lived up to the crowd's excitement. In his first season with the team, he scored an average of 23.4 points per game. A goal scored in basketball earns two or three points. This means that Shaq scored about eleven **baskets** per game.

Shaq was also good at blocking and rebounds. He grabbed an average of 13.9 rebounds per game. He played so well that after his first week on a **professional** court, he was named Player of the Week. He was the first **rookie** in NBA history to make such a big splash so quickly.

Shaq with his mother Lucille O'Neal. Lucille is a big inspiration in Shaq's life. Here they proudly show off the Chic Boutique Spirit Award she won, given every year to deserving African American women.

Early Years

Basketball superstar Shaquille Rashaun O'Neal (pronounced sha-KEEL ra-SHAWN oh-NEEL) was born in Newark, New Jersey, on March 6, 1972, to Lucille O'Neal. His father, Joe Toney, left the new family. Lucille, raising her baby son alone, gave him her last name. His first two names come from a book of Arabic names. They mean "Little Warrior." But Shaquille quickly took the nickname Shaq (pronounced SHAK), and still uses it.

Lucille O'Neal and Philip Harrison, who worked for the city of Newark, met and fell in love. Soon Shaq had a stepfather who loved him as well. Shaq thinks of him as his real father. Shaq has two younger sisters, Lateefah (lah-TEE-fah) and Ayesha (eye-EE-shah), and a brother, Jamal.

When Shaq was very young, both of his parents worked. They had a tough time earning enough money. When Shaq was two, Philip Harrison joined the U.S. Army. The army promised him a steady **salary**, but it meant that the family would have to move. The army sends its soldiers to many places.

While Shaq was in the first grade, his family moved to an army base in Bayonne, New Jersey. Shaq didn't have time to make many real friends. In the third grade, Shaq's father was ordered to move to another army base. This one was in Eatontown, New Jersey. Then, once again before Shaq could make any new friends, the family was sent to an army base in Georgia.

By this time Shaq was almost ten years old. He was taller and bigger than the other boys on the base. They made fun of him because of his size. They called him names. Shaq got into a lot of fights trying to stop them.

His father told Shaq, "Be proud of being that size. One day, you'll see."

Shaquille O'Neal dunks the ball for two points while Sacramento Kings forward Michael Smith attempts to catch the falling ball. Shaq hasn't yet let go of the rim of the hoop.

Shaq poses with his former college basketball coach Dale Brown. When Shaq was a teenager, Brown taught him how to play basketball like a professional. This picture was taken during Shaq's graduation ceremony at Louisiana State University in December 2000.

Basketball Pro

Philip Harrison and his family were sent to Germany. They stayed there long enough for Shaq to make friends with a German boy named Mitch Riles. They both liked to play basketball, and they liked to pretend to be real basketball stars.

By the time Shaq was thirteen, he was six and a half feet tall. He wore size 17 shoes. Dale Brown was the **head coach** of the Louisiana State University basketball team. He was in Germany looking for new players. Brown thought that Shaq was a soldier! He was surprised to learn that Shaq was only thirteen. He liked Shaq and trained him to play basketball like a **professional**.

Shaq battles with Matt Geiger of the Miami Heat, trying to shoot a basket. Geiger is trying to block him. After this play, Shaq finds out that he's badly strained his thumb, but it heals.

When Shaq was fifteen, his family moved to an army base in San Antonio, Texas. Shaq went to high school there. He was on the school's basketball team. Shaq was still growing, and he was already very strong. When Shaq made a **slam dunk**, jamming the ball through the **basket**, he bent the rim of the hoop. He was a very good player, though, so no one got angry.

In 1989, Shaq graduated from high school. He went to Louisiana State University. He had grown to an inch over seven feet tall, shoe size 22, but he could move quickly. He was so good at college basketball that he was named Player of the Year.

The NBA stands for the National Basketball Association. **Scouts** from NBA teams saw Shaq play. On June 24, 1992, a Florida team called the Orlando Magic picked Shaq to join them. Now he knew that his father had been right. He could be proud of his size.

Shaquille O'Neal (right) tries to get Nick Anderson (left) fired up during a game against the Detroit Pistons in Orlando.

Champion

At only nineteen years old, Shaq was suddenly very rich. He had signed a seven-year contract with the Orlando Magic for $41 million. He also was chosen by two companies, the sneaker maker Reebok and the soft drink giant Pepsi, to do **endorsements**. This means Shaq would appear in commercials for them. The **endorsements** earned him even more money.

One of the first things that Shaq did was buy some nice things for his family. He didn't go crazy about spending, though. As he says, "with money and fame came responsibilities," and he knew he should help those in need. Shaq decided to help **charity** organizations like the United Way. Later, he started the Quality of Life fund. It helps nursing students pay for school.

He also didn't let the Orlando Magic down. Shaq played so well that first year with the Magic that he was named 1993 **Rookie** of the Year.

In August 1994, Shaq played on the U.S. team for the World Basketball Championship, held in Toronto, Canada. He helped the U.S. team win.

The biggest goal for a **professional** basketball team is to win the NBA Championship. In the spring of 1995, Shaq's skills helped the Orlando Magic get as far as the NBA Finals. They didn't win the championship, but that was closer than they had ever gotten before.

Shaq did want to win the championship, though. On July 18, 1996, he moved from that team to the Los Angeles Lakers. He thought the Lakers had a better chance of winning the championship. His seven-year contract with them paid $120 million.

On October 29, 1996, Shaq was honored as one of the Fifty Greatest Players in NBA

This photograph was taken from above. It gives a new look at Shaq leaping up to score a basket. Players from the New Jersey Nets can't stop him.

history. But early that season he was injured. He hurt his leg and missed about half of his first year with the Lakers. In 1998 and 1999, he came back and again was one of the NBA's best players.

On June 19, 2000, Shaq led the Lakers to an NBA Championship. They repeated the win in 2001.

In 2004, Shaquille O'Neal was traded to another team, the Miami Heat.

Shaq tries to take the ball away from Los Angeles Laker player Kobe Bryant. But instead, he causes a foul. The Lakers get two free shots.

New York Knicks player Kurt Thomas tries to stop Shaquille O'Neal. But Shaq moves around him, blocking him. Shaq goes on to score.

Shaq and his wife Shaunie take their children to the Los Angeles Premiere of Shrek 2. Shaq tries to spend as much time as he can with his kids. He loves being a dad.

Father, Actor, and Rapper

As a **center** in basketball, Shaq makes use of his size and quickness. He's too big to make **jump shots**, the ones in which players leap up into the air to throw the ball into the **basket**. Instead, he scores most of his points with **slam dunks**. He's also very good at blocking the shots of the other team. He's very difficult to stop. Shaq does have one weakness, though. He isn't very good at free throws.

Shaq is busy away from basketball, too. On December 15, 2000, he finally earned his college degree. He said, "It didn't seem right to me to be telling kids to stay in school when I hadn't gotten my degree."

On December 26, 2002, Shaq married his longtime girlfriend, Shaunie Nelson. They have

Here is Shaquille O'Neal the rap musician. He has recorded four CDs of his music. But he is still much better known as a basketball star.

three children together: Shareef Rashaun, Amirah Sanaa, and Shaquir Rashaun. Shaq also has another daughter, Taahirah, who was born in 1996 to Arnetta Yardborough. He also dotes on Myles, Shaunie's son from a previous relationship. Shaq says family is his most prized possession. "I'm a friendly dad. I love to play with my kids and tickle them," he said. ". . . Being around them feels better than winning an NBA championship."

Shaq has also acted in eight movies, although none of them was very successful. (He has appeared as himself in many others.) He has a record label and is known as a rap artist. Shaq has also written three books, *Shaq Attaq!*, *Shaq Talks Back,* and a children's book, *Shaq and the Beanstalk and Other Very Tall Tales.*

Shaq does not take drugs or smoke. He thanks his parents for bringing him up right. He sponsors a yearly event called the Shaqtacular to raise money for poor children. His shoe company makes sneakers that do not cost as much as many other brands.

Shaq also participates in the Nestle Crunch Hot Shots Camp for kids. The camp is open to winners of a nationwide contest for teens with the best basketball skills. The winners get to go one-on-one with Shaq and learn the moves that make him such a great player. They also join him for a private lunch.

On March 16, 2005, Shaq had his picture printed on the Wheaties box. Wheaties cereal is nicknamed "The Breakfast of Champions." Since 1934, kids have grown up seeing sports stars on boxes of Wheaties. Shaq is no exception. "I grew up idolizing the great athletes who were on the Wheaties box," he said. "That's why it's such an honor for me to become part of the Wheaties family."

So far, Shaq's first year with the Miami Heat has been a good one, even if he hasn't broken any records. How does he expect to keep doing in Miami? Shaq says, "I don't have anything to prove to people. However, I do have something to prove to myself. Right now I have a few [championship] rings, but when I'm done I want six or seven."

Robbie Tripp (right) was one of the winners who got to go to the Sixth Annual Nestle Crunch Hot Shots Camp. He got to play basketball with Shaquille O'Neal. But here Shaq is clowning around to make everyone laugh.

For many years, Wheaties has recognized outstanding athletes by putting their pictures on special cereal boxes. In this picture taken in 2005, Shaq stands next to a giant box of Wheaties that has his photo on the front. He is proud to have been chosen for this honor.

1972 Shaquille O'Neal is born on March 6.

1985 Thirteen-year-old Shaq is trained in Germany by U.S. basketball coach Dale Brown.

1989 Shaq graduates from Cole High School after leading its basketball team to two winning seasons.

1991 At Louisiana State University, Shaq is named basketball Player of the Year.

1992 Shaq is picked by the Orlando Magic to play professional basketball. He is named NBA Player of the Week, the first such award to a rookie after his first week of play.

1993 Shaq is named to the NBA All-Star Game and wins Rookie of the Year. His first book, *Shaq Attaq!,* is published in October.

1994 At the World Basketball Championship in August, Shaq helps the U.S. team win the gold medal. He stars in his first feature film, *Blue Chips.*

1995 Shaq is top scorer in the NBA and takes the Orlando Magic to the NBA finals.

1996 Shaq wins a gold medal at the Olympic Games. On July 18, he signs with a new team, the Los Angeles Lakers. Forms his record label, TWIsM (The World Is Mine). First daughter, Taahirah, is born to Arnetta Yardborough.

2000 Shaq and the Lakers win the NBA Championship. Shaq earns his college degree.

2001 Shaq and the Lakers win a second NBA Championship.

2002 Shaq marries Shaunie Nelson on December 26. They have three children: Shareef Rashaun, Amirah Sanaa, and Shaquir Rashaun.

2004 Shaq is traded to the Miami Heat.

2005 Shaq is honored to have his picture printed on the Wheaties cereal box.

SELECTED DISCOGRAPHY

Shaq Diesel, 1993
Shaq-Fu: Da Return, 1994
You Can't Stop the Reign, 1996
Respect, 1998

SELECTED FILMOGRAPHY

Blue Chips, 1994, starring Nick Nolte and Shaquille O'Neal in a basketball drama.

Kazaam, 1996, starring Shaquille O'Neal and Francis Capra in a fantasy about a genie and a lonely little boy.

Steel, 1997, starring Shaquille O'Neal and Annabeth Gish, in a fantasy adventure based on a superhero comic book character.

Year of the Yao, 2005, starring Shaquille O'Neal and Yao Ming in a "docudrama," a documentary about the Chinese basketball star.

CAREER SHOOTING STATS

YEAR	TEAM	G	MIN	FG	FGA	FT	FTA	PTS	AVG
1992-93	ORL	81	3071	733	1304	427	721	1893	23.4
1993-94	ORL	81	3224	953	1591	471	850	2377	29.3
1994-95	ORL	79	2923	930	1594	455	854	2315	29.3
1995-96	ORL	54	1946	592	1033	249	511	1434	26.6
1996-97	LA-L	51	1941	552	991	232	479	1336	26.2
1997-98	LA-L	60	2175	670	1147	359	681	1699	28.3
1998-99	LA-L	49	1705	510	885	269	498	1289	26.3
1999-00	LA-L	79	3163	956	1665	432	824	2344	29.7
2000-01	LA-L	74	2924	813	1422	499	972	2125	28.7
2001-02	LA-L	67	2422	712	1229	398	717	1822	27.2
2002-03	LA-L	67	2535	695	1211	451	725	1841	27.5
2003-04	LA-L	67	2464	554	948	331	676	1439	21.5
2004-05	MIA	70	2407	636	1061	339	731	1611	23.0
TOTAL		**879**	**32900**	**9306**	**16081**	**4912**	**9239**	**23525**	**26.8**

FIND OUT MORE

Books and Articles

Barker, Barbara. "Big Kid in a New Playground," *Newsday,*
October 31, 2004.

Spencer, Lyle. *NBA Superstar Shaquille O'Neal.* New York:
Scholastic Books, 2002.

O'Neal, Shaquille. *Shaq and the Beanstalk and Other Very
Tall Tales.* New York: Hyperion/Jump at the Sun, 1999.

Web Addresses

NBA Player Profile: "Shaquille O'Neal"
http://www.nba.com/playerfile/shaquille_oneal/
index.html

Sports Illustrated Scrapbook: "Shaquille O'Neal"
http://sportsillustrated.cnn.com/basketball/nba/features/
shaq/scrapbook/main/

The Sun-Sentinel, "Shaq Central"
http://www.sun-sentinel.com/sports/basketball/heat/shaq/

Works Cited

Christian, Charlie. *Shaquille O'Neal.* New York: Barnes &
Noble Books, 2003.

Christopher, Matt. *On the Court With . . . Shaquille O'Neal.*
Boston: Little, Brown & Company, 2003.

Kaufman, Michelle. "Lion King." *Miami Herald,* October 31,
2004. http://www.miami.com/mld/miamiherald/
sports/special_packages/basketball_preview/
10040949.htm

O'Neal, Shaquille, with Jack McCallum. *Shaq Attaq!* New
York: Hyperion Books, 1993.

_____. *Shaq Talks Back.* New York: St. Martin's Press,
2001.

Rappoport, Kevin. *Shaquille O'Neal.* New York: Walker &
Company, 1994.

basket—in basketball, the hoop through which a ball must pass to score points.

center—a position in basketball that keeps the player close to the center of the court.

charities—organizations that help people in need.

coach—in sports, the person who teaches the sport.

endorsement (en-DORS-munt)—the support of a product by a famous person.

head coach—the person who leads a team.

jump shot—in basketball, leaping into the air to throw the ball toward the basket and into the hoop.

make a basket—to score points in basketball by getting the ball through the hoop.

professional (pruh-FEH-shuh-nuhl)—someone who is paid to do a job.

rookie (RUH-kee)—in sports, someone playing in his or her first year with a league.

salary (SAH-luh-ree)—a set amount of pay for a job.

scout—in sports, a person who looks for new players for a team.

slam dunk—a way of making a basket by jumping up and shoving the ball through the basket.

Brown, Dale 12, 13

Harrison, Philip 9, 10, 13

Los Angeles Lakers Win NBA Championship 20

Miami Heat 14, 20, 26

NBA (National Basketball Association) 7, 15, 19, 20

Nestle Crunch Hot Shots Camp 26, 27

O'Neal, Lucille (mother) 8

O'Neal, Shaquille

As rapper 24, 25

Attends Louisiana State University 12, 15

Birth 9

Books 25

Brother (Jamal) 10

Children (Shareef, Amirah, Shaquir, Taahirah, Myles) 25

Does endorsements 17

Honored One of Fifty Greatest Players 19

Joins Los Angeles Lakers 16

Marries Shaunie 23

Named NBA Player of the Week 7

Named Rookie of the Year 19

On Wheaties box 26, 27

Picked by Orlando Magic 5

Sisters (Lateefah, Ayesha) 10

Starts Quality of Life fund 17

Traded to Miami Heat 20

Orlando Magic 5, 7, 15, 16, 17, 19

Riles, Mitch 13

Shaq Attack 5

Shaqtacular 25

Toney, Joe 9

United Way 17

World Basketball Championship 19

Yardborough, Arnetta 25